WORSHIP
& MUSIC MINISTRY

by Rick Ryan & Dave Newton

THE WORD
FOR TODAY
PO Box 8000 Costa Mesa CA 92628

Worship and Music Ministry
by Rick Ryan and Dave Newton
General Editor: Chuck Smith

Published by **The Word For Today**
P.O. Box 8000, Costa Mesa, CA 92628
Web site: http://www.thewordfortoday.org

ISBN 0–936728–63–9

© 1995 The Word For Today

Except where otherwise indicated, all Scripture quotations are taken from the New American Standard Bible, © 1960, 1963, 1968, 1971, 1972, 1973, 1975, 1977, by the Lockman Foundation. Used by permission.

TABLE OF CONTENTS

Preface

When Luke wrote the message of the gospel to Theophilus, he declared that his desire was to set forth in order a declaration of those things that are most surely believed among us. Luke desired that Theophilus might know the certainty of those things in which he had been instructed.

We seem to be living in a day of spiritual confusion. Paul wrote to the Ephesians that they not be as children, tossed to and fro with every wind of doctrine by the slight of men and the cunning craftiness whereby they lie in wait to deceive. Because of all the confusion in the church today, and the many winds of doctrine that continue to blow through the body of Christ, we felt that it would be good to have various pastors write booklets that would address the issues and give to you the solid biblical basis of what we believe and why we believe it.

Our purpose is that the spiritual house that you build will be set upon the solid foundation of the eternal Word of God, thus we know that it can withstand the fiercest storms.

Pastor Chuck Smith
Calvary Chapel of Costa Mesa, California

INTRODUCTION
BEGIN WITH GOD'S WORD

God's Word encourages believers to abound in all things, including faith, utterance, knowledge, and the earnestness of love (2 Corinthians 8). The premise of this book is that it is very worthwhile to abound in a scriptural knowledge of worship, and that this will carry over into music ministry and the life of the church. The Greek words used for knowledge are *gnosis, suneido,* and *akouo.* The gnosis is often used by Luke to connote the scientific knowledge gained through observation of facts that lead to firm conclusions. The suneido speaks of finally becoming aware of something or to have something brought to your attention. And the akouo (the root of our word "acoustic") means to hear and comprehend, or understand.

Together, these three words for knowledge and understanding appear over 450 times in the New Testament. There is much to be known, and much that God wants us to understand. These verses include the *gnosis* of many specific areas (e.g., God, salvation, mysteries, and the Law). The Bible does say that knowledge will one day be done away with (1 Corinthians 13:8), and that, in comparison, love is far better than knowledge (1 Corinthians 13:2). And, once we are with Christ for eternity, there will no longer be a need for man's interpretations of the Scriptures, because then we will know in full, whereas now we only know in part (1 Corinthians 13:12).

But it also states that knowledge is manifested in those who believe, as a sweet aroma of God's victory in Christ (2 Corinthians 2:14), and that God's true knowledge is different from that which the world promotes (1 Corinthians 3:19). Just as there were many first century Christians who were noble-minded in the city of Berea, may God richly bless you as you are prompted to carefully examine His Word for His truth in these matters that pertain to worship (Acts 17:11).

CHAPTER 1
WORSHIP AND BIBLICAL TRUTH

The first principle for worship and music ministry is that: ***Knowing Biblical Truth Will Cause People to Worship God.*** David said that the Word of God is upright (Psalm 33:4). Knowing God's Word is the basis for the ministry, because the Word of God is a lamp to the believer's feet and a light to his path (Psalm 119:105). As a person grows in understanding and knowledge of God's Word, an awareness of God's love, and God's great plan of salvation, the most natural outcome will be a strong desire to give worship, praise, and thanksgiving to the Lord. David declared, "Your Word I have treasured in my heart that I might not sin against You" (Psalm 119:11). Knowing God, His love, and His plan of salvation, together serve to equip the church for ministry in the world.

A second principle is that: ***The Same Care Given to the Teaching of God's Word Should Also Be Given to the Worship of God***. During a typical church service, a large portion of the time is given over to the teaching from God's Word and to the worship of God. Tremendous care must be taken to ensure that this time is rich and meaningful in the life of the church body, and fruitful in its entirety. As people focus their attention on the true and living God, they will give praise and blessing to the Lord. Psalm 95:6 states that man is to come and worship, to bow down and kneel before the Lord his Maker; and Psalm 63:3–4 continues that because God's lovingkindness is better than life, so our lips will praise Him, and we will bless Him, and lift up our hands to His name.

It is an awesome responsibility to lead others in the worship of God. The heart of a worship leader should be like that of a pastor; humble in spirit, submissive to the Lord, and filled with the Holy Spirit (Hebrews 13:17). One pastor stated that what is needed in church leaders is a heart with passion and compassion;

that is a passion for knowing God and a compassion for people. The Scriptures support this (e.g., Deuteronomy 30:10; Psalm 25:6; 51:10; 72:13). Pastors and worship leaders should each have a strong desire to know God (Deuteronomy 4:29; Proverbs 8:17), and this must be combined with a sincere heart for individual people (John 15:17; 1 Peter 1:22). The ministry of worship is to exhibit a pure love for God and this will produce good fruit in the lives of believers.

Chapter 2
Worship and Church Life

Worship is defined as devotion and reverence, adoration and admiration. The word is used over 160 times in the Bible, and the acts of worship (singing praises, clapping hands, bowing down, giving thanks) are mentioned together more than 600 times. The word used for worship in the original text means to cherish, to laud, or to extol. The third principle is clear: ***God Alone Is Worthy of Our Worship.***

God is the only One uniquely qualified and worthy to be worshipped by man (Exodus 34:14; Psalm 81:9). The reason that God is worthy to be worshipped is that He created everything that is, and there is no one more powerful than Him. The Bible states very clearly, "Worthy are You, our Lord and our God, to receive glory and honor and power; for You did create all things, and because of Your will they existed, and were created" (Revelation 4:11). In Deuteronomy 6:4, the great Shema called Israel to worship the One true God. Jehovah also gave man His ten commandments, in which He clearly requires that man shall have no other gods before Him because He is a jealous God (Exodus 20:3–5), and because He is the One true God, man should not take the name of the Lord in vain (Exodus 20:7). In Matthew 4:10, Jesus correctly referred men to the basic principle that they are to worship the Lord God alone, alluding back to the great Shema of Deuteronomy chapter 6.

It has been said that some sports fans worship their favorite team, or their favorite athlete. Some musicians are worshipped by their adoring public. A man has even been known to worship his fully-restored classic automobile. There must be a biblical basis for the way that God should be worshipped.

Worship is that act of completely giving over one's interest, desires, and admiration to some other person or thing. David declared by the Holy Spirit that a zeal for God's house had "consumed" him (Psalm 69:9). That is the essence of true worship, to be totally consumed with our Lord. People will worship someone or something, whether explicitly by intention, or implicitly relative to the time made available for related activities. A person's attention will have a definite focus.

Someone once said that a person's love, worship, and commitment to God could be observed in their planning calendar and their checkbook.

How Do We Worship?

It is clear that God wants man to worship Him, but *how* is God to be worshipped? In today's church, the word "music" is often freely substituted for the idea of "worship"; however, music is not necessarily synonymous, or automatically interchangeable with, the idea of worship. People will often say, "It's time to worship" and what they mean is that it is time to begin singing. But, music is merely one form or means by which individuals can act on and express their worship to God. The substantive content of worship does not change, but there are many different ways in which worship of God is manifested through the actions of individuals.

Sometimes worship is accomplished by bowing low (Psalm 95:6). In other accounts, worship is done in holy array and in trembling (1 Chronicles 16:29–30; Psalm 96:9). It is shown by those who put their face flat to the ground (2 Chronicles 20:18), by those who dance (Psalm 149:3), by others who clap their hands and shout (Psalm 47:1), and those who sing joyfully (e.g., Psalm 9:11). Still other places in Scripture speak of being still before God and meditating in the heart (Psalm 4:4; Isaiah 30:15), or being silent before the Lord (Psalm 65:1). There are also descriptions of people lifting up their hands to the Lord (Psalms 63:4; 119:48) and even those who lift up their hands to God while at the same time bowing their faces low to the ground (Nehemiah 8:6). It is comforting to know that there is not just one way or position by which man can worship God; but there remains only one basis for worship.

There are numerous accounts throughout the Scriptures of people worshipping God. The Old Testament summarizes more than 100 instances, and the New Testament over 50 episodes, of people bowing down to worship God. Yet the one constant in each of these

accounts is that it is only God who is worthy to
be worshipped.

Jesus is fully God, and as such He was
worthy to accept the worship of others. He was
worshipped while still a small child when the
Magi came about one year after His birth
(Matthew 2:11). He was worshipped in a boat by
His disciples (Matthew 14:33). He received the
worship of many others as well as a blind man
(John 9:38), a Samaritan leper (Matthew 8:2;
Mark 1:40), a synagogue official named Jairus
(Matthew 9:18; Mark 5:22), a man possessed by
demons (Mark 5:6), a Canaanite woman
(Matthew 15:25), a repentant prostitute (Luke
7:38), a Syrophoenician woman (Mark 7:25),
Lazarus' sister Mary (John 12:3), and others after
His resurrection (Matthew 28:9,17).

It is quite interesting to note just how few
details are given in the gospels about explicit
instructions of *how* to worship Jesus. Often those
who worshipped Jesus were "amazed" or "in
awe"; they were "intrigued" and "wondering"
as they pondered the Lord, and then bowed
before Him and worshipped. Once, after Jesus
had healed a lame man, the multitudes who had

witnessed it were filled with awe, and then glorified God (Matthew 9:8).

The worship of God might be summarized in the following manner. First, worship can be done through thoughts (Psalm 16:7), feelings or emotions (Psalm 9:1), and desires that God can actually place inside a man (Psalm 37:4). It is the spirit of man that longs to know the God who created him in His own image. Next, there are then outward manifestations of thoughts, feelings, and desires. These are the actions or deeds that one does (Psalm 33:15; Matthew 5:16). The Bible usually refers to these as works. Words that are spoken are one form of an outward manifestation of the Spirit inside man. Verbal expression can be directed to, or about God. Words can also take the form of verse or rhyming prose to express thoughts, feelings, and desires of the heart toward God. Music is a natural medium by which a man can express in words his sincere worship of God.

Our Basis for Worship

The fourth principle is to: *Worship God in Spirit and in Truth.* The Bible teaches that worship is not so much the position of the body, as it is the posture of the heart. The concept of worship can only be discussed once a clear understanding of God is established. In the first epistle to Timothy, an exhortation is given for Christians to remember a basic truth, that God dwells in unapproachable light (chapter 6:15–16). In both the first chapter of John's gospel (John 1:4) and the first chapter of John's epistle (1 John 1:5), the Holy Spirit plainly witnesses that God is light, and in Him there is no darkness at all. Over 60 times in the New Testament believers are referred to as those who are made full of His light. God is not contained in a physical space. He exists in Spirit, outside of time and space. John's gospel clearly states that God Himself is Spirit, and those who desire to worship Him *must* do so in spirit and in truth (chapter 4:23–24).

This same concept is clearly expressed to the church in Philippi when Paul states that true worship is not accomplished in the flesh, but only in the spirit (chapter 3:3). Conversely, God's Word teaches that worship can also be in vain. The Lord states clearly that for some, worship is done with words only. This is paying lip service alone to God while a person's heart remains far from God. This type of reverence consists merely of traditions that were learned and repeated by rote memory (Isaiah 29:13), and is not true worship of God.

There is a biblical basis by which the content of worship can be judged. Although there is room for different styles of worship, there is no room for different substance (content) of worship. The Bible teaches that true worship must entail these two components: it must be *in spirit* and *in truth*, together. This could be represented by four different combinations in the life of a person. A person must ask both, "Is my worship in the spirit?" and "Is my worship in truth?" If the answer to each of these is "yes" (position number 1), it would be obvious that the worship is pleasing and acceptable to God; just as if the answer to both of these were "no" (position number 2), it would be obvious that the worship is not.

But, what of the other two possible combinations? Many individuals may answer "yes" to the first question (they believe that they are worshipping in spirit) and yet what transpires in this time is *not* true relative to God's Word (position 3). And others may have their doctrine and actions all in order so that they would state that they worship God in truth, but yet they may do so in the flesh and not in the spirit (position 4).

If the worship that is offered is only offered in one's spirit, then the lack of truth becomes the basis by which the worship is summed up and found lacking. If someone has all their "doctrinal ducks in a row" but lacks the spiritual component, there is again a lacking in the sum content of the worship.

This does not mean that it is time to start categorizing churches or even individuals; but it does provide a basis by which a person could ask in the quietness of their own heart whether they are truly in that place where they can worship God as He has commanded. If one of the two components is missing, then there is a biblical basis by which to admonish the substance of worship.

True worship cannot simply be in spirit alone, just as it cannot be only based on possessing correct doctrine. True worship is in spirit *and* in truth.

Can Worship Be in Vain?

During His ministry, Jesus proclaimed that it was possible for worship to be in vain

(Matthew 15:9; Mark 7:7). The vanity that He referred to was that there were those who purported that the ideas and rituals for worship that had been devised and instituted by men were being taught as if they were clear scriptural doctrine. Jesus called these *entalma anthropos* (in the Greek), which literally means "commands of men."

Men had decided what was necessary to worship God and had substituted their own ideas for the true worship of God. In Matthew 15:6, Jesus clarified what had happened by stating that men had in fact "invalidated" the Word of God. The word He used was *akuru*, which was used in that day to speak of an annulment of a contract. It meant more than simply that the contract was broken, but it went further back to declare that the initial contract itself had never been valid in the first place. This is the same idea by which some churches will declare a marriage to be annulled; it is not like a divorce that breaks and seeks to end a marriage contract. It actually renders null and void the initial marriage vows themselves as though they had never happened in the first place. The "religious" hierarchy of that day had invalidated God's Word by substituting a litany of man-made rituals, recitations, and postures in place of the true worship of God.

These passages make it clear to the church today that it is possible for man to be, at times, misguided or misdirected in worship; that a person could bring worship to God in an inappropriate manner. Two simple components serve as prerequisites for a person who wants to worship God; worship is done in *spirit* and in *truth*.

Perhaps one of the worst realizations for an individual would be to learn that one's worship of God was in vain, that it was useless, that it counted for nothing. It would be quite shocking to people if there were a device to walk through as they left a church service, much like the metal detectors at airports. Could you imagine if it could measure the sincerity and authenticity of the worship that had just been offered to God? Remember, we do not worship God simply because it makes us feel good. The prayers and praises of God's people go up to God like a fragrant aroma (Exodus 30:9; Leviticus 16; Psalm 141:2; and Revelation 5:8). God has said that the true precepts of the Lord can sometimes be heard by men merely as a "sensual song," like one who has a beautiful voice and plays well on an instrument; the words are heard, but are not abided by those who hear (Ezekiel 33:32). Yes, worship can make a person feel very good, but the reason for worship is to please the Lord (Psalm 104:34).

Remembering Who We Worship

Perhaps this is an appropriate place to remember that our worship is directed toward the Lord of the universe. He is the beginning and the end, the creator of all things. There is a need for man to be reminded that the fear of the Lord is clean, enduring forever (Psalm 19:9) and that the fear of the Lord is the beginning of wisdom (Psalm 111:10). The Holy Spirit said, "Come, you children, listen to me; I will teach you the fear of the Lord" (Psalm 34:11). It is imperative that people take a moment, prior to a time in worship, to remember *who* it is that they are going to worship. Certainly God has made provision for man to come before the throne of God with confidence through His Son, Jesus Christ. Hebrews 4:16 says, "Let us therefore draw near with confidence to the throne of grace, that we may receive mercy and may find grace to help in time of need." But, the delicate balance is that we can both address Him as Father (sometimes *pater* in the Greek, meaning father or parent, and other times *abba* meaning dad), yet be always aware that He is the one who impartially judges according to each man's work, so we should conduct ourselves in that fear during the time of our stay upon the earth (1 Peter 1:17).

It has become quite popular in many churches to conclude a song of worship with a rousing applause. Indeed, the Bible declares that "the trees of the field will clap their hands" (Isaiah 55:12) and, "clap your hands, all peoples; shout to God with the voice of joy" (Psalm 47:1). Yet, some worship leaders will lead the congregation with the remark, "Let's all give the Lord a big hand this morning." For an unbeliever, or someone very new in their walk with Christ, this may create an impression that the Lord is simply a good performer who we clap for, in the same way that an entertainer receives applause from the audience. "Giving God a hand" can tend to trivialize the magnificent power and awesome nature of God.

This is not to say that worship should always be done in a trembling manner, laying prostrate on the floor before God. This is also not to conclude that any clapping is wrong or inappropriate. But 1 Peter 1:17 is an excellent reminder of the balance we need to have in how we approach and address the Lord of the universe.

Some churches today tend to have a more informal atmosphere in their church services when compared to many traditional denominations that practice a formal liturgy during their services. This relaxed atmosphere can make it easy to bring unbelievers to church to hear the gospel message. However, the church should not become nonchalant in its regard of the awesome attributes of God. If during our worship, the spiritual veil could be drawn open for us to catch a glimpse of God ruling and reigning from His throne in heaven, it is quite probable that "giving God a hand" would severely understate the awe and reverence that His throne should rightfully command.

John (in the Book of Revelation) and Ezekiel (in the Old Testament) were privileged to be given an audience into the heavenly realm. Isaiah gave an incredible account of his experience (Isaiah chapter 6) seeing the Lord on the throne, high and lifted up, with seraphim attending Him. For each of these men it was a similarly overwhelming experience, such that it was nearly more than they were able to take in.

Some applause during worship services has also been misunderstood by many in the congregation to be directed toward the worship leader and the accompanying music team. A young man who was very new in his relationship with Christ once commented that he came to the service to "hear the band play" and when it was good, he loved to applaud, much like at a rock concert. Worship before the Lord must never be confused with a concert atmosphere, where musicians are performers who become the focus of the congregation's attention. These and other spiritual issues related to worship leaders and musicians are dealt with in chapter four.

It is crucial to always remember who God is. This provides a clear rationale for the intentions that support the worship of God. The Bible states that God is the everlasting Lord and Creator of the ends of the earth (Isaiah 40:28). It also provides a clear picture of God's attributes, that He is eternally pre-existent, with no beginning or end (Revelation 22:13). He is not contained within the realm of time (Deuteronomy 33:27), so God is also omnipresent (Psalm 36:5; 71:19; 108:4). He exists as Spirit and is not bound by physical or spatial parameters. God is uniquely omniscient; He knows all there is to know about everything in the universe because He created it all Himself (Job 28:23–24; Psalm 44:21; 94:11). He is also omnipotent; He has more power than anything in His created universe (Isaiah 29:15–16; Amos 9:6). It is God, Himself, who holds the very fabric of the universe together (Psalm 95:5). This is the God whom we worship.

Man's Desire for God

There is a strong yearning in the heart of man to have fellowship with, and know, God. The psalmist rightly said that as the deer pants for the water brooks, so his soul panted for God; that his soul thirsted for God, for the living God. He asked when would the day finally come when he would be able to appear before God in person (Psalm 42:1–2). In Romans chapter 8 and in 2 Corinthians 5, the Holy Spirit witnesses that there is a deep longing inside man to be clothed in that which is eternal, to be fully redeemed. The Bible teaches that the spirit of man is the lamp of the Lord, searching all the innermost parts of man's very being (Proverbs 20:27). David sang that only one thing would he desire from the Lord, and that he would seek; that he might dwell in the house of the Lord all the days of his life, and behold the beauty of the Lord and meditate in His temple (Psalm 27:4). He also wrote of his deep inner desire to be with the Lord (Psalm 38:9). He realized that there is no one else in heaven for him but the Lord, and besides the Lord he desires nothing. He continues that his flesh and his heart may fail, but God is the strength of his heart and will be his portion forever (Psalm 73:25–26).

Revelation 4 states that the Lord God is worthy to receive glory and honor and power; for He created all things, and because of His will they existed, and were created in the first place. The Bible teaches that God takes pleasure in His people (Psalm 149:4) and that He is at work within man to will and work His good pleasure (Philippians 2:13).

Man has always possessed a desire to search for God. There is a hunger deep within the soul

of man to know God (Psalm 84:2). But it is also
clear that it is God who meets man, and that
apart from God, there can be no satisfying of
man's desire and longing to know God and be at
peace with Him (Psalm 145:16). God has said
that money cannot buy that which man needs to
be satisfied and whole (Isaiah 55:2). Jesus even
commented to the woman at the well that she
worshipped that which she did not know (John
4:22). Paul recognized that the people of Athens
were ignorant in their worship, searching for the
one deity they could not idolize in their statues,
in their altar to "an unknown God" (Acts 17:22–
23). Perhaps the history of religion in the world
can be summed up as the various efforts and
attempts of man to find and know God. But the
story of Jesus Christ is God's plan to reach out to
man, to reveal Himself and to make Himself
known to man in a personal relationship. And
that certainly is the good news.

Worship God Alone

The Bible recounts numerous instances
where someone other than the one true God was
the focus of worship. When worship is given to
someone besides God, the consequences are
disastrous. Much of the Old Testament speaks of

Israel's constant rejection of Jehovah for false gods.

Jacob understood God's displeasure with the worship of false gods, so he instructed his entire household to put them away and to purify themselves before God (Genesis 35:2). There is defilement, uncleanness, even perversion that comes when worship is given over to someone or something other than God. Jehovah warned Moses and Israel that the worship of other gods would be a snare to them (Exodus 23:33). The Lord later declares that He is the God of gods and the Lord of lords, the great, the mighty, and the awesome God (Deuteronomy 10:17).

Satan attempted to persuade Jesus to worship him, but Jesus rebuked him that only God can be worshipped (Matthew 4:9–10). When the Roman Cornelius received Christ as Savior, he attempted to worship Peter, but was quickly admonished that worship is not to be directed toward a man, but only toward God (Acts 10:26). When John was nearly finished experiencing the Revelation given to him by Jesus Christ, he tried to worship the angel envoy that had shown him so many things that were to take place. As John bowed to worship him, this messenger quickly admonished John by saying, "Do not do that; I am a fellow servant of yours, your brethren the prophets, and those who heed the words in this book; worship God" (Revelation 22:9). Notice how he finished this statement, with the truth about worship; he told John to *worship God*.

In a similar manner, Paul had to admonish one church to turn away from their worship of angels (Colossians 2:18). The believers in Colossae had turned their attention to the messengers of God rather than to God Himself. Once again, man had invalidated the true worship of God and replaced it with a practice that was contrived by men. Even today, there are churches that teach the worship of angels.

Some churches allow worship to be directed to men who have already died, or toward the Virgin Mary. Still other church congregations worship physical artifacts such as holy water or eternal lamp oil that are believed to contain special powers of healing and restoration. Many well intending individuals venture every year to certain towns, cathedrals, fields, mountain tops, and tombs, to catch a glimpse of some apparition or to bow before some religious relic.

They believe that these locations and objects are somehow more directly and intentionally linked to God. Pictures, statues, icons, and vestiges do not hear, they cannot see, and they will not respond to the worship and prayers of man. The Lord has said, "Woe to him who says to a piece of wood, 'Awake!' and to a dumb stone, 'Arise!'; that is your teacher? Behold, it is overlaid with gold and silver and there is no breath at all inside it" (Habakkuk 2:19). Remember, idols of silver and gold are the work of man's hands. They have mouths, but they cannot speak; they have eyes, but they cannot see; they have ears, but they cannot hear; they have noses, but they cannot smell; they have hands, but they cannot feel; they have feet, but they cannot walk; they cannot make a sound with their throat... and those who make them and trust in them will become like them (Psalm 115:4–8).

Some people even worship the physical pages of the Scriptures, keeping the "good book" displayed on a pedestal, with special illumination. Perhaps the angel's commentary to John in Revelation is the best word for the church today concerning worship, namely "worship God."

CHAPTER 3

WORSHIP AND MUSIC

The letter to the Ephesian church has a clear and comprehensive exhortation for every Christian. In chapter five, the Holy Spirit instructs believers to be careful in the way in which they walk. Their walk should be as one who is wise. This infers that it is contrasted to a walk that is *un*wise. The rationale for this posture is that by walking wisely, individuals can redeem the time allotted to them on the earth, and that this is necessary because man's days are inherently evil. It continues that man is to not be filled with wine (which is earthly), because this type of filling puts a person's mind in a state of dissipation (meaning literally to scatter or disperse). Rather, the one who is aware of the need for a redemption of their time

on the earth should be filled with the Holy
Spirit.

Psalms, Hymns, and Spiritual Songs

The fifth chapter continues that when a
person is not dissipated (scattered), he or she
can then speak to other people clearly through
several means. The first manner is through
psalms. This Hebrew word, *psallein*, literally
means "to pluck strings." The Greek word used
is *psalmos*, which literally means "to move an
instrument."

Musical instruments are one means by
which a person can express worship to God.
This same principle is also taught in Colossians
3:16, where believers are encouraged to have the
Word of Christ richly dwell within them, with
all wisdom and teaching, admonishing one
another with psalms, hymns, and spiritual
songs, and singing with thankfulness in their
hearts to God. Believers are to come before the
Lord's presence with thanksgiving and to shout
joyfully to Him with psalms (Psalm 95:2).

In 1 Chronicles 16, some of the Levites were
specifically assigned to minister (worship)
before the ark of the covenant in celebration,

praise, and thanks with harps, lyres, and loud-sounding cymbals. Later, in 2 Chronicles 5, the trumpeters and the singers were to be heard with one voice and to praise and glorify the Lord when they lifted up their voices accompanied by trumpets and cymbals and instruments of music. Psalm 150:4 says to praise Him with timbrel, dancing, stringed instruments, and pipe.

The second means described in both Ephesians and Colossians shows that man can also communicate with hymns when filled with the Holy Spirit. The Greek word is *humnos*, which literally means "praise of God." Nehemiah made sure that at the dedication of the wall of Jerusalem the Levites were brought to Jerusalem so that they might celebrate the dedication with gladness, with hymns of thanksgiving and with songs to the accompaniment of cymbals, harps, and lyres (Nehemiah 12:27). A hymn is generally directed as praise to God. In Acts 16, it is recorded that Paul and Silas were sitting up around midnight, praying and singing hymns of "praise to God," and the prisoners were listening to them.

The third type of music mentioned in Ephesians and Colossians is the "spiritual song," or literally "a taunt that comes directly from the Holy Spirit." This taunt is a very interesting concept. In the Greek it is called the *pneumatikos oide*, a spiritual or supernatural composition. This could describe music that is given as a gift by the Holy Spirit for the edification of the church body.

The structure of this term speaks of music inspired by God "through man's spirit" for the Holy Spirit to communicate truths to man for the building up of the saints. The passage in Colossians 3:16 provides the context for these songs; they are for *teaching* and *admonition*. The prior verse establishes that for this music, the peace of Christ rules in the believer's heart, and that we are part of the one body of Christ, always giving thanks. In the same manner, verse 20 of the Ephesians passage describes the context of this music as being in the body of Christ and giving thanks to God.

The fifth principle is that: *The Holy Spirit Has Gifted Us With Music for Worship.* These three types of communication: psalms, hymns, and spiritual songs, are then placed in the broader context that they are accomplished by singing and making melody with the heart. In the Greek, making melody with "the heart" is literally *kardia*. This means that the melody is made with one's very being, thoughts, and feelings. The context is further clarified to incorporate an awareness to be always giving thanks for all things in the name of the Lord. This whole process also includes a condition that believers who participate in these are subject to one another in the fear of Christ. This is quite reassuring and provides the necessary form of accountability (the checks and balances) by which a person can know that what transpires is good and truly from God.

Psalm 98:5–6 speaks of making melody with the lyre, trumpets, and the sound of horns. Psalm 107:22 says that the great works of God should be told through joyous singing. Moses sang, "The Lord is my song" (Exodus 15:2). In all the heavenly scenes told of in the Bible, music and singing are always present. In Revelation 5, those from every tribe, tongue, people, and nation are singing in concert together before the throne of God. Later, in Revelation 14, those people who come out of the tribulation are singing their own special song before the throne.

In Revelation 15, one of Moses' songs makes the "play list" of heaven as those who overcome the Antichrist sing his song and play golden harps on a sea of glass.

Man's Desire to Worship God

Man has a deep inner desire to know fulfillment. There are many things that people pursue (and use) to try and obtain fulfillment. This longing encompasses a need to express feelings and thoughts and desires. This is consistent with the creative attribute of God by which man was formed, and the creativity that then exists in each man.

There are various ways in which man's heart and desires can be expressed in an outward fashion. Some spoken means of expression would include poetry and verse, different styles of prose, narratives, prayers, novels, instrumental melodies, and songs with lyrics. Music is one of the different formats by which man can express feelings, desires, hope, peace, joy, and love toward God. A song is a vehicle to convey thoughts and feelings of the heart. Music is a gift of expression given to man by God.

David proclaimed that the Lord put a new song in his mouth, a song of praise such that many will see and fear and will trust in the Lord (Psalm 40:3). David knew that the Lord was his strength and his shield and he trusted in Him; therefore his heart exulted the Lord with a song to thank Him (Psalm 28:7). God is the one who puts the song in man. The song is always there for man to express a heart of love and praise toward God. David also said that he remembered his song in the night, and that he used this song to meditate with his heart and to allow his spirit to ponder the things of the Lord (Psalm 77:6). David said, "I will sing a new song to Thee, O God upon a harp of ten strings I will sing praises" (Psalm 144:9). In heaven, some of the singing before the Lord's throne is of familiar songs (Revelation 15:3), and some is with new songs that God gives His people (Revelation 5:9).

Isaiah knew where his songs came from. He clearly stated, "I will trust and not be afraid for the Lord God is my strength and my song and He has become my salvation" (Isaiah 12:2). In the very same way, Moses also knew that the Lord God was the author of his songs (Exodus 15:2). Ezekiel even stated that God's Word to

Israel was like a beautiful song, except that the people did not hear and obey the instruction to them in the lyrics (Ezekiel 33:32). Zephaniah wrote that the Lord will rejoice over His people with singing (Zephaniah 3:17).

The following is a sampling from the Psalms of the way that music and song come together as integral parts of the worship of God. David wrote, "I will sing to the Lord, because He has dealt bountifully with me" (Psalm 13:6). "Sing to the Lord a new song; sing to the Lord, all the earth" (Psalm 96:1). "Sing to the Lord, bless His name; proclaim good tidings of His salvation from day to day" (Psalm 96:2). "O sing to the Lord a new song, for He has done wonderful things, His right hand and His holy arm have gained the victory for Him" (Psalm 98:1).

"Serve the Lord with gladness; come before Him with joyful singing" (Psalm 100:2). "I will sing to the Lord as long as I live; I will sing praise to my God while I have my being" (Psalm 104:33). "Sing to the Lord with thanksgiving; sing praises to our God on the lyre" (Psalm 147:7). "Praise the Lord! Sing to the Lord a new song, and His praise in the congregation of the godly ones" (Psalm 149:1). "Let everything that has breath praise the Lord" (Psalm 150:6).

"Worship the Lord with reverence, and rejoice with trembling" (Psalm 2:11). "Who may ascend into the hill of the Lord, and who may stand in His holy place? He who has clean hands and a pure heart" (Psalm 24:3–4), "So purify me with hyssop, and I shall be clean; wash me, and I shall be whiter than snow" (Psalm 51:7). "All the earth will worship Thee, and will sing praises to Thee; they will sing praises to Thy name" (Psalm 66:4). "Come, let us worship and bow down; let us kneel before the Lord our God our Maker" (Psalm 95:6). "Exalt the Lord our God, and worship at His feet; for the Lord our God He is Holy" (Psalm 99:5).

The Holy Spirit made a promise as He guided David to begin the Book of Psalms: How blessed is the man who does not walk in the counsel of the wicked, nor stand in the path of sinners, nor sit in the seat of scoffers; but his delight is in the Law of the Lord; and in His Law he will meditate, every night and every day. And he will be just like a tree firmly planted by the streams of water; the yield will be the fruit in its season and blessing in whatever he may do

(Psalm 1:1–3). The Bible is clear that God uses music and song for worship and praise.

CHAPTER 4
WORSHIP LEADERS IN THE CHURCH

The sixth principle for worship and music ministry is that: *God Has Called Worship Leaders to Serve the Body of Christ.* Is there a biblical definition for a "musician"? Although there does not exist one particular Scripture passage with a four-point outline of God's description of a musician, there are several references to music and musicians that can, when taken together in their entirety, provide a firm foundation upon which music and musicians can be defined and more closely understood.

An Old Testament Basis

Psalm 100 states that man is to serve the Lord with gladness, and that when coming before the Lord it should be done with joyful singing. Israel had men who were specifically called to be leaders in this area of singing. It is very interesting to note that in the Bible, of the more than 125 references to singing, singers, and songs, over 85 percent of these are in the direct context of joy and gladness. Perhaps the starting place for a biblical definition is that a musician is first and foremost a person full of joy and gladness.

In 1 Chronicles 15:22, Chenaniah (chief of the Levites) was placed in charge of the singing. Why was he given this position of music leader? It says that he gave instruction in singing because he was skillful. The Lord had gifted him for the very purpose that he might lead God's people in singing praises.

Later on, in 1 Chronicles 25, a music ministry is described under the direction of a man named Heman, along with two other worship leaders, Asaph and Jeduthun. There were 288 musicians and singers under the direction of Heman to sing in the house of the Lord with cymbals, harps, and lyres for the service of the house of God. The three worship leaders were then under the direction of the king. This was quite a music ministry: three leaders under the authority of the king, and under them were nearly 300 musicians who were called specifically because they were gifted in music. It also explains that they cast lots among themselves to decide when each would fulfill their music service before the Lord. They were organized into 24 separate music teams, perhaps to cover 6 days per week (not including the Sabbath day) in each cycle of 4 weeks for their appointed music ministry before the Lord.

In a nearly identical manner, 1 Chronicles 6 describes how David also had a worship team that was selected to lead the singing and praises of God. They were "appointed over the service of song." These men led the music at the tabernacle until the temple was completed and they served "according to their order." These accounts recognize those who are uniquely gifted of God to serve as leaders in worship.

A third, very similar, passage in Scripture explains how, when the walls of Jerusalem were finally reconstructed and ready for the dedication ceremony, Nehemiah called the five Levites to oversee one of the most tremendous praise and worship services ever recorded in the

Bible, which would be accompanied by cymbals, harps, and lyres (Nehemiah 12:27). Jeshua, Binnui, Kadmiel, Sherebiah, and Judah then appointed Mattaniah as the musician in charge of the songs of thanksgiving along with his brothers (Nehemiah 12:8). The skilled singers and musicians were then divided into two huge choirs, one standing all along the top of the wall to the left of the city gate and the other on the right. The worship music went up before God and was so loud it could be heard from afar. Nehemiah then explains that in the days of David and Asaph, there were leaders of the singers, songs of praise, and hymns of thanksgiving to God (Nehemiah 12:47). God ordained that there were those specifically called to serve Him as worship leaders. They were skillful in their abilities as they served the Lord.

The seventh principle is that: *The Worship of God Is Service to God.* Is a gifted musician automatically qualified as a worship leader? There is a noticeable difference between a person gifted in music and a *worship leader*. Worship leaders may in fact be gifted musicians, but not all gifted musicians are qualified to be worship leaders.

Musical Gifts and Service

A *worship leader* does more than simply lead other people in singing songs. The time spent in congregational worship should be led by a spiritually mature individual who is gifted with both a right heart that is motivated by God with a love for Him and for people, and then musical ability. The word in the Bible for "worship" is translated "to minister," or "to serve." A servant is one who ministers, or one who worships. The Greek word for servant is *diakonos*, which literally means an attendant. Throughout the Bible, the term "servant" is used to describe a person who attends to another, and this is often used to describe someone who ministers and someone who worships. Over two-thirds of the references for service, servant, and to serve are in the context of joy, gladness, or rejoicing. Dozens of passages speak of those who serve with joyful singing, who sang in their service to God, or servants who brought their song before the Lord.

The Gospel of Matthew makes a particular case that the rulers of the Gentiles lord their position over those who are under their authority; this is contrasted by the idea that

Christians are instructed to *be different* from this practice. The Holy Spirit wants believers to know that whoever wishes to become great, shall first be a servant, a *diakonos*, an attendant. In chapter 23, Matthew clarifies the fact that the greatest shall be the servant. Mark's Gospel recounts that Jesus told the twelve disciples that if anyone wants to be first, he shall be last, and servant of all. Certainly, being a servant does not carry with it a prominent position in this life. Romans 13:3–6 also discusses this same idea about those placed in authority.

Servant Leaders

Musicians who are worship leaders are really servant (service) leaders. They are placed in a position to serve the body of Christ when the congregation comes together to worship (serve) the Lord. The attention is focused on the Lord and not on the musician leading the worship. The church body does not gather together to praise the worship leader. This attitude of "service" is needed, so it is important to clarify *who* it is that is served. The Bible clearly teaches that the only one worthy to be served is the Lord God.

Several passages point to two reasons that the Lord is the one who should be served. First, He is served because we love Him, so we are glad to do it; we desire to do it (Psalm 100:2). Second, He is served because He has first served us, and provided an example for service. This idea of service through example is found in Mark 10 where, the Son of Man did not come to be served, but to serve, and to give His life a ransom for many.

There is great reward in taking on the position of a servant. John 12:26 records that if anyone serves the Lord, that person should be prepared to completely follow the Lord. This posture puts the servant in a place where Jesus commented that where He (Jesus) is, there shall His servant also be; so that if anyone serves the Lord, the Father will honor him. That is an amazing statement; that the Father will honor a man who serves the Lord. Paul seemed to understand this prospect. He told the Ephesian church that he had been made a servant, according to the gift of God's grace which was given to him according to the working of God's power. So not only does the Father honor the servant of the Lord, but it is only by the working of God's power that a person can even be a servant in the first place.

The Bible refers numerous times to a certain type of servant, a bond slave. The Greek word for this type of servant is *doulos*. The clear distinction in this term is that the servant is willing to serve. This is not forced labor, where a slave serves a master under duress. The bond servant chooses to serve through an intentional act of his own volition.

How Do We Serve in Worship?

The next logical question should be focused on *how* we serve. Paul urged the Christians in Rome to present their bodies as a living and holy sacrifice, acceptable to God, because it was their spiritual service of "worship." There was a clear understanding that being a servant was first and foremost *spiritual* in nature, and jointly related to the worship of God.

When a person accepts Christ as Savior, the earthly body has then become the temple (the dwelling place) for the Holy Spirit (1 Corinthians 6:19–20). God has commanded that worship should be *in spirit* and *in truth*. God dwelt among Israel in the first temple which was the tabernacle, or "tent of meeting" (Exodus 40:34). He often filled the tabernacle with His presence. It is only through the indwelling and filling of the temple of man by the Holy Spirit that one can truly worship God. Specific issues related to worship and the Holy Spirit are covered in chapter six.

Worship Leaders and Identity

Worship of God provides an opportunity for man to further develop an identity, a true relationship, with God. However, there can be a tendency on the part of individuals to identify themselves solely (and uniquely) in the context of their service within the church. Think of the pastor who normally receives a good deal of attention and may be rather reluctant to give up that recognition to a guest speaker. The same can occur with worship leaders. The musician's identity has become so enmeshed in the role of worship leader, that it becomes difficult to not be the one leading the congregation in the worship portion of the service. It is probably a good idea to require that worship leaders have designated times to *not* lead worship, but to sit among the general congregation and be led in worship by others.

There is a tremendous work God can do in a worship leader's heart during time away from center-stage. Some churches find it refreshing to use more than one worship leader scheduled on a rotating basis throughout the church's monthly calendar of worship services. These leaders can then also work with a larger pool of gifted musicians from within the church body. This format of having more than one worship leader and music team has the additional benefit of opening up greater opportunities for more people to serve in the music ministry of the church, removing the exclusivity that could be associated with a sole leader and only one music team. True service should never be pursued relative to a personal need to be included or active in a certain role. Service in music ministry must only be viewed as service toward God and to Him alone.

In a similar way, people in the congregation should not begin to migrate toward a certain individual worship leader as the basis upon which they involve themselves in music ministry. Paul made it clear that a person is first given an opportunity to serve, and that this opportunity comes from the Lord (1 Corinthians 3:5). However, some are quick to attach their

ministry position to an individual, just as many
Corinthians had begun to identify themselves
with either Paul or Apollos. The Holy Spirit's
admonition to that church was, "What then is
Apollos, and what is Paul; servants through
whom you believed, even as the Lord gave
opportunity to each one." Paul knew he planted
seeds of the gospel and that Apollos watered,
but it was God who caused the growth. So it is
in worship. One person may encourage a deeper
level of worship and another inspire worship
through their musical gifts, but it is God who is
worshipped.

This should encourage those in music
ministry. People in the church body should not
look to any ministry leader for their sustenance,
because it is neither the one who plants nor the
one who waters that truly matters, but it is God
who causes the growth. The person who plants
and the person who waters are similar; but each
will receive his own reward according to his
own labor.

Paul took this idea one step further in his
second letter to the church at Corinth. He wrote
that a person is not adequate in and of himself to
consider anything (of spiritual value) as coming

from himself. Rather that for each of us, our adequacy is from God alone, who also made each of us adequate as servants of a new covenant, not of the letter, but of the Spirit. Why? Because the letter kills, but the Spirit gives life (2 Corinthians 3:5–6).

A person must have recognizable gifts from God to accomplish the ministry that God gives to him or her. Some people may have a passion for God and a compassion for people, yet not be gifted to teach the Word of God, or to effectively lead a congregation, and impart a vision for the church. Their love for God and for people do not, in and of themselves, qualify them for the position of pastor-teacher (Romans 11:29; 12:6–8). God must gift them in that area.

In the same way, a person with a sincere heart for ministry may not be gifted by the Holy Spirit to lead others in worship, and may not be gifted musically. Would such a person be a good fit as a worship leader? Probably not. The opposite also holds true. An individual may be a good speaker, have tremendous knowledge of God's Word, and may even have that dynamic personality to lead other people. This person may have also earned a graduate degree from a seminary and be very intellectual. But if the heart of this person has no passion for God, or compassion for people, the outward traits by themselves cannot qualify this individual to be a pastor.

So it is for worship leaders as well. A person could be an extremely well-accomplished musician or composer, play several instruments professionally, and have a beautiful solo voice, but if that person's heart does not have the qualities of love, service, and humility, then the outward abilities alone cannot qualify this person to be a worship leader.

Serving on God's Behalf

Those in worship music ministry do act on behalf of God in front of the church body, as well as in front of those who are unbelievers. Paul further encouraged those serving in ministry to give no cause for offense in anything, in order that the ministry not be discredited, but in everything be commending ourselves as servants of God (1 Corinthians 10:32–33). This was not only to include the good and desirable aspects of ministry service, but was specifically tied to those situations where an individual would need much endurance in times of affliction, hardships, and distress (2 Corinthians 6:4–8). He even noted that this could include beatings and possible imprisonment.

The list of willing situations was quite long and went on to involve tumults, labors, even sleeplessness and hunger. These were all to be counted as "normal" circumstances for those who would be servants. These were then to be handled in purity, knowledge, patience, and kindness, in the Holy Spirit, and in genuine love. I wonder how many people serving in music ministry would be prepared to truly suffer hardship for the Lord as a component of their service.

WORSHIP AND THE WORD OF GOD

In that music is a very personal expression of an individual's thoughts about someone or something, there can be a tendency for Christian songwriters to incorporate their own understandings of God, His love, and His salvation into their lyrics. This, in and of itself, is not wrong, however, there must be a standard for truth against which all ideas about God are compared when used in musical compositions. The eighth principle is that: *Worship Should Be Wholly Consistent With the Teaching From God's Word.*

Lyrics should exhibit truth in both substance and accuracy relative to God's own Word. The Bible is the only source by which lyric content can be properly evaluated. This is not to say that every songwriter is then limited to only arrange Bible verses to music. God's creative nature is certainly alive in man. But man's mind is not always God's mind, and man's ideas are not always consistent with God's truth.

This is not intended to be a blanket critique of the entire community of contemporary Christian composers. However, just as it would be wrong to limit song lyrics to Bible verses alone, it would be equally misguided to simply allow personal freedom of expression to reign as the sole basis for discerning the lyrical content of original compositions. The music that is written within the church body for praise and worship must be held to a standard in the same way that the content of a pastor's sermon must teach true doctrine in a manner consistent with God's Word.

Three Categories of Music

We propose that there are three basic categories of music in the church. The first deals with those songs whose lyrics are directed toward God. These are worship songs of praise, adoration, and thanksgiving sung directly to the Lord. The second type are those whose lyrics are directed to others in the body of Christ. These are songs of testimony and encouragement, songs of inspiration and edification for those who hear. The third category includes songs with lyrics that carry the message of the gospel to those who do not yet know Jesus Christ as Savior. This is music of evangelism, with a message for a lost world. There is no specific place in Scripture that teaches this, but these three categories do provide a framework to include all the music in the church.

Yesterday and Today

Songs of praise and worship to God should clearly exhibit basic truths about who God is. There should be a recognition that worship can be directed to the Father, Jesus Christ the Son, and the Holy Spirit. Some of the classic hymns of the 18th and 19th centuries were composed with lyrics that were doctrinal feasts. They were comprised of four or five verses that generally read (and sang) like New Testament commentaries, Bible dictionaries, and concordances. Many of today's older denominations take great pride in the heritage and content of these "great hymns of the faith."

The more recent history of the church (the last 25 years) has witnessed a virtual explosion of new "contemporary" songs of praise and worship. In the same way, many of today's younger *non*denominational churches take great pride in the identity that these songs have created for newer church bodies. The older denominations tend to worship with older hymns accompanied by a piano or an organ. The newer *non*denominational church tends to worship with contemporary praise music (often referred to as "praise choruses") accompanied by acoustic and electric guitars, bass, drums, as well as piano and organ (but they are now electric and referred to as "keyboards").

The newer churches desired to break out of the shadow of the older churches. Older denominational churches were widely regarded by the *non*denominational churches as spiritually dead, so the music was "upgraded" to better fit the times. As rock 'n' roll burst on the scene in the late 1950's and grew in popularity during the 1960's and 1970's, the newer nondenominational churches deliberately moved away from anything that was a reminder of the traditional and liturgical "high church."

Gone were the ornate altars, the candles, the pews, the stained glass, and the long robes for the pastors and choir. Gone too, was the idea that the congregation could only worship God in a two-piece suit and tie, or a dress and high heels. Gone were the recitations of creeds, memorized formal prayers, and the traditional form of worship, namely hymns accompanied by a piano or organ. The formality of the church would be replaced by a new *in*formality. Each person embraced the encouragement of that classic hymn and decided to come to church "just as I am." Men's hairstyles and sideburns got longer and the dress code was rewritten as casual. In the same way that the secular music captured the hearts of the public, the new contemporary praise and worship music captured the hearts of people who wanted to approach God and worship Him in a way that they could better relate to.

The church embraced the rhythms and instruments of the secular world, perhaps inspired by Larry Norman's lyrics, "Why should the Devil have all the good music?" The chronology of the musical growth that followed has been well-documented in other books. In summary, an entire industry of contemporary Christian music was born. The new music filled all three of those categories mentioned at the start of this chapter. There were contemporary songs for the praise and worship of God. There were songs of testimony and encouragement for the church body. And there were songs (and bands) to take the gospel message to an unbelieving world.

When the newer churches moved away from the traditional church service format, the implicit (and sometimes explicit) commentary on the traditional format was that it was no longer relevant or meaningful. It was dead. However, there was nothing wrong with the hymns and the organ. What was lacking was the vibrancy with which the church had originally introduced this music during the great revivals and spiritual awakenings of the 18th and 19th centuries. The life behind the melodies and lyrics had not died, the hearts of the people had grown cold.

It would be backward to think that the tremendous spiritual awakening among America's youth during the 1970's was brought about by contemporary music. The opposite is true. The move of God's Spirit on these young people brought about a new heart and attitude of revival in the music and format of the church.

It was not the music that moved God's Spirit, it was God's Spirit that moved the music.

Exclusive Music?

Based on the growth of the new music in the church, a dangerous polarization of worship has been created between the traditional format with hymns, and the contemporary format with its own music. In the same way that the modern churches announced that the new music was "theirs," the traditional churches proclaimed that the 100 year-old hymns were theirs. What has followed are unfortunate instances of divisiveness within the body of Christ. It was not enough to have doctrinal differences between denominations, but now there exist praise and worship dissimilarities as well.

The two extreme ends of the continuum are as follows: the traditional churches somewhat sarcastically refer to contemporary worship music as simply "praise choruses," the implication being that they are light in content and doctrine, but heavy in experience and feelings. (The notion being that the vast majority of modern praise and worship music is little more than short, repetitive choruses for the spiritually immature to sing around the campfire at summer camp.) On the other hand, the contemporary *non*denominational church derisively refers to traditional hymns as "outdated," implying that they are monotonous and laborious to sing. These people say they cannot "connect" their thoughts toward God because the lyric content is so formal and heavy, while the words and melodies lack personal feeling. (The notion here is that they are stuffy, overly-intricate expressions of doctrine written in minor keys for the spiritually catatonic to recite by candlelight, accompanied by a bellowing pipe organ.)

The ninth principle is that: ***Worship May Allow for Differences in Style, but the Substance and Content Should Always Be the Same.*** People may indeed have a preference toward a particular style or tempo of music. Certain musical arrangements may more personally "connect" with some people versus another music or lyric style. There should never be an adversarial relationship between traditional hymns and contemporary praise and worship music based upon tempo or instrumental arrangements.

Different personal preferences in style allow for a wide range of musical expression to be focused toward the Lord. Christians in the Baltic-Republics might prefer an up-tempo mandolin played in a minor key while a congregation in Iowa favors a Wesleyan hymn accompanied by organ and piano. Believers in northern Peru love to worship to fast strumming guitars and tambourines while the church in Nairobi may prefer an a cappella chorus backed by various drums and instruments of percussion. All these various styles bring songs of praise and worship to God. John observed the worship in heaven before the throne of God to include those from every tribe, tongue, people, and nation (Revelation 5:9). The musical style of worship may vary but the content must never sway from the truth revealed in the Bible.

Content, Style, and the Holy Spirit

By excluding the other's form of music and worship from its own agenda, both ends of the continuum are equally guilty of extremism. A church body can be vibrant and spiritually alive singing hymns with an organ, and a congregation can be dismal and spiritually dead singing contemporary praise music with a ten-piece band and a state-of-the-art sound system. There is music written in the "hymn" format that is light in doctrinal content and there is contemporary praise music that is rich in scriptural truths. To sum up, there are great hymns and bad hymns; there are great contemporary praise songs and really poor praise songs.

It would be wrong to think that only the hymns of the last 200 years can be used of God, and that He cannot use contemporary praise and worship music. It is equally incorrect to believe that only contemporary praise and worship music is valid for today and that the great hymns of the past are no longer relevant for God to use in the church. Today, contemporary composers have sought to move beyond the traditional hymns of the 18th and 19th centuries in the same way that the hymns were once "contemporary praise music" and moved beyond the traditional Gregorian chants that they replaced. It is very probable that 25 years from now, when the children of today have grown, they may be writing lyrics and composing praise music that will be quite different in style from the contemporary music of today.

If the Lord should tarry beyond the year 2020, the music of the 1970's will be over 50 years old and may at that time be referred to as "traditional" music. If this sounds as though it could not happen, think about the last time you were in a doctor's waiting room and heard an "easy listening" radio station play a violin version of one of your favorite rock anthems from the 1960's. Music styles vary across both time and geographic boundaries, but the Word of the Lord never changes (1 Peter 1:25).

The church should seek an atmosphere of balance; a place where hymns and contemporary praise music can joyfully coexist. That is not to say that hymns of rich content must find a home with feeling-oriented praise music. Rather, that hymns and contemporary praise music, both rich in content and expressive in love and honor for God, would come together in a sweet union of past and present melodies and style, neither taking precedence to the exclusion of the other. In the church service there are together elements of formality and a casualness that welcome everyone to come and worship at Jesus' feet and hear from His Word.

Chuck Girard sang of that "little" Calvary Chapel on the edge of town having people with long-hair, short-hair, and some coats and ties. It was very plain to see, that people were not the way they used to be. What was most significant however, was that people were "coming around" to the understanding that the body of Christ is made up of many different people. The preacher was not talking about "religion" anymore, he just wanted to praise the Lord. The people were not stuffy like they were before, they too just wanted to praise the Lord. That one "little" church now ministers to an excess of 30,000 people per week, and has raised up more than 700 separate churches throughout the world.

God moved in a mighty way in Europe and in the U.S. during various parts of the 18th and 19th centuries. It was not the worship music that caused revival in the church, it was the moving of the Holy Spirit in people's hearts. The traditional hymns sung in churches today were once the contemporary praise and worship music of that era.

In those times, many Christian composers adapted biblically-based lyrics to fit the style of music of their day. During the Reformation in Europe, a former Catholic priest wrote lyrics about God's great power and might and adapted these to a catchy tune that was very popular in the taverns across Germany. Today, that former piece of 16th century "contemporary Christian praise and worship music" has become the "traditional" hymn of Martin Luther, "A Mighty Fortress Is Our God."

Consistency in Content

Worship leaders who stand or sit at a microphone in front of the congregation are similar to pastors at a pulpit. The worship leader is placed in a prominent position before the assembly of the church body and is able to greatly impact people by what is sung, spoken, and communicated by actions. The lyrics of the songs and the words of the prayers offered together have the capacity to influence a great number of people. It is imperative that everything they proclaim have no variation from biblical truth.

When the songs, the prayers, and the sermon come together in the truth of God's Word, each of these components of the church service supports and substantiates each other.

The lyrics that the congregation sings forth are entirely consistent with the Word of God. The prayers that are offered are also completely in line with God's Word. And, finally the teaching is an exposition without deviation from God's Word. Adherence to God's Word creates a unanimity between worship, time in prayer, and the sermon during the service.

Without such cohesion of content, the service would send mixed signals to the congregation, which will only contribute to confusion. The people in the congregation are then left in an awkward position. They will either recognize the inconsistencies, or they will not. If they are able to discern variations from what they know is in God's Word, the credibility of the church leaders could be called into question.

The biggest concern, however, is for those who are not capable of dividing truth from error. Those who are new in their faith, or those who have not thoroughly studied God's Word are naive and very impressionable as they sit under the direction of church leaders. They can easily begin to build their own theology much like someone sews a patchwork quilt. The final product is nothing more than a collage of many different positions joined by a common thread of unsuspecting immaturity, naiveté, and ignorance.

Watching Over Worship

Jesus warned His disciples to be on their guard because various stumbling blocks would come in among God's people (Luke 17:1–2). Elders were instituted by God to serve as those who would oversee the content and conduct of the church body (1 Timothy 3:1–7). The early church was charged to be sure that these overseers were to serve as shepherds to guard the flock (the people in the church) against those who would come in to rob (Acts 20:28). Jesus referred to Satan as the thief who comes only to steal, kill, and destroy (John 10:10).

Sometimes the enemy may come against the church with an obvious frontal attack. More often the deceiver comes into the church through very subtle means that, to the undiscerning eye, do not appear to be invidious. Satan would like nothing better than to infiltrate the church through the music and lyrics of the worship of God. There have been many well-publicized cases of elders calling into correction

pastors who strayed from the truth of God's
Word. But it is not as well known how many
elder boards have kept a close doctrinal vigil to
watch over the content of lyrics as offered to the
church body by the worship leader. Worship
music should be wholly consistent with the
Word of God.

Chapter 6
Worship and Spiritual Warfare

The tenth principle is perhaps the one that deals with the greatest controversies in the church today: *Worship Is a Spiritual Matter so it Will Definitely Encounter Spiritual Warfare in the Church.* The Holy Spirit instructs the church that the weapons of our warfare are not of the flesh, but divinely powerful for the destruction of fortresses, destroying speculations and every lofty thing raised up against the knowledge of God, and taking every thought captive to the obedience of Jesus Christ (2 Corinthians 10:4–5). When our eyes are off the Lord, and when our priorities and agenda are different from His, then confusion, bewilderment, and turmoil replace the order and understanding that comes from God.

It is important for Christians to be reminded of several spiritual truths from God's Word. First, the peace of God surpasses all comprehension and guards your heart and mind in Jesus Christ (Philippians 4:7). Second, remember that our struggle is not against flesh and blood, but against the rulers, powers, and world forces of darkness, and against the spiritual forces of wickedness in the heavenly places (Ephesians 6:12). Worship and the Word of God have continually been those two areas where the enemy has focused his assault against those who truly believe in God.

The Enemy's Contradictions

Satan denied and contradicted God's Word when he tempted Eve in the garden (Genesis 3) and when he tempted Christ in the wilderness (Matthew 4). The enemy wants to disrupt the worship of God. The Bible explains that Satan held the position of God's worship leader in the heavenly realm until his heart coveted and desired the position of God, His glory and praise. He wanted the glory and honor and praise for himself. He also told Eve that she could be "just like God," and he has been spreading the same lie to mankind ever since. In this same way, man is inherently sinful, always pondering in his heart the lust of the flesh, the lust of the eye, and the boastful pride of life (1 John 2:16).

Jesus rightfully compared the attitude of the hearts of two men who went into the temple to pray and worship before God. One was a prideful Pharisee boasting in his own high regard of himself. The other was a humbled publican (a tax collector) aware of his sin and broken before the Lord. Jesus stated clearly that the publican was the only one who went out of the temple justified, because those who exalt themselves will be humbled, but those who humble themselves will be exalted (Luke 18:10–14). The very thing that caused Satan to rebel against God and fall into sin was his desire to exalt himself. This remains a primary stumbling block for the church today. Sin causes the focus and attention to be taken away from God, and placed on someone else.

The Enemy's Aspirations

In Isaiah 14, the writer moves into a spiritual realm with a word for the former choir director of heaven. Beginning in verse 9, the Word of the Lord describes a heavenly creature who has become like the kings of the earth who have been laid low in Sheol (the abode of the dead). Verse 11 states that this individual's pomp (ceremony) and the music from his harp have been brought down to a place of maggots and worms, a place of decay where there is no life. Verse 12 further clarifies this individual's identity as the "star of the morning" and "the son of the dawn." This is obviously not the earthly king in Mesopotamia, but the spiritual entity behind the king's power and actions.

The reason this heavenly being was brought down begins to unfold in verses 13 and 14 where he boasts in his heart five different times that "I will..." Each of these boasts are in relation to obtaining something that is not his own, but that which belongs inherently to God alone. First he states, "*I will* ascend to heaven." Second he states, "*I will* raise my throne above the stars of God." Third he boasts, "*I will* sit on the mount of assembly in the recesses of the north." Fourth, he states, "*I will* ascend above the heights of the clouds." Finally, he remarks, "*I will* make myself like the Most High." God immediately responds to these covetous statements in verse 15, declaring that in spite of his aspirations, he will still be thrust down (by force) to the abode of the dead.

This same creature is also spoken of in a very similar manner in Ezekiel 28:12. The prophet speaks to the spiritual entity behind the king of Tyre. This creature had the seal of perfection, was full of wisdom, and perfect in beauty. Verse 13 states that this same being was in the garden of Eden (the king of Tyre had not been in Eden, but Satan had). The Lord continues to explain that every precious stone was his covering: the ruby, the topaz, the diamond, the beryl, the onyx, the jasper, the lapis lazuli, the turquoise, and the emerald.

Perhaps verse 14 is the most provocative in that the Lord discloses that this creature was titled "the anointed cherub who covers." God placed this being on the holy mountain of God, and he walked in the midst of the stones of fire. This magnificent being was blameless in his ways from the day he was created until unrighteousness was found in him. Verses 16 through 18 state that he was responsible for the Lord's sanctuary, as one who was anointed to cover the worship of God. But this beauty and splendor, inherent in the position of worship leader, turned out to be the basis for his fall as pride swelled up and the star of the morning became covetous of the position and glory of the Lord God. Verse 17 says that he corrupted his wisdom by reason of his splendor.

In his pre-fall condition, Satan was the most beautiful being of God's creation. His close proximity to the Lord proved to be more than he could handle. Isaiah 14 records that he wanted what the Lord had, and who the Lord was, for himself. The Hebrew word in Ezekiel 28:12 refers to him as *haylel*, the "star of the morning," also translated Lucifer. He is referred to 14 times in the Old Testament as "Satan" and in Genesis chapter 3 as the "serpent," the same serpent from Revelation 12:9.

The Enemy's Deception

The church has been warned to see to it that no one takes it captive through philosophy and empty deception, according to the tradition of men, according to the elementary principles of the world, rather than according to Christ (Colossians 2:8). Satan operates a deception of wickedness with power and signs and false wonders (2 Thessalonians 2:9–10). Christians can be sure that he will use his power and craft against spiritual matters within the church.

Dissension and hindrances will find their way into the church through deception (Romans 16:17–18). John made it clear that the reason he wrote the truths of God was because there were those who were trying to deceive the church (1 John 2:26) and this was the work of the Devil (1 John 3:7–8). When Satan is thrown into the abyss at Christ's second coming into Jerusalem, God Himself declares that the reason for this incarceration period is that Satan will then no longer be able to deceive the nations (Revelation 20:3). The ultimate deception of Satan is how he exchanges the truth of God for a lie, so as to worship and serve the creature rather than the Creator (Romans 1:25).

Deception simply means "to represent something that is counterfeit as if it were true." This is the purpose of Satan's efforts toward believers. Obvious lies are immediately recognized by Christians as fake. But the Devil often works in very subtle ways that are not obvious in order to introduce falsehood into the church. The Holy Spirit made sure that the church would know that Satan is capable of disguising himself as an angel of light (2 Corinthians 11:14). His craft is the ability to take that which is false and present it in such a way that it has the appearance of truth.

Turns from the truth that are most subtle, are those that are most difficult to discern. God wants believers to be able to discern falsehood from truth. God's Word is the true basis by which a lie can be discerned. Why? Because the Word of God is living and active and sharper than any two-edged sword, piercing as far as the division of soul and spirit, of both joints and marrow, and able to judge the thoughts and intentions of the heart (Hebrews 4:12).

The solid food of the Bible is for the spiritually mature who, because of practice, have their senses trained to discern good and evil (Hebrews 5:14). Christians are to abound still more and more in real knowledge and all discernment, so that they may approve the things that are excellent, in order to be sincere and blameless until the day of Christ (Philippians 1:9–10). That is probably why one of the primary gifts of the Holy Spirit is that of discerning (or distinguishing) spirits (1 Corinthians 12:10). God knows that man must be supernaturally empowered to differentiate the truth from a lie.

The eleventh principle is that: ***Worship of God Will Not Hinder or Contradict God's Word.*** Deception can even infiltrate the worship of God. The Lord has clearly stated that worship is to be in spirit and in truth. Satan can introduce a lack of truth into worship through words and actions that are false, that do not have a biblical basis as truth. Many activities take place in the church under the category of worship that are totally false. Churches often like to take out of context a single event or reference from the Bible and construct an entire doctrine around this activity.

The Roman guards placed at Jesus' tomb fell down "as dead men" when the angel appeared like lightning (Matthew 28:4–5). This passage has been expanded and embellished into the practice of believers being "slain in the spirit," an act of collapsing backward onto the floor during worship due to the power of God. Many churches focus the worship time not so much on God as they do on experiencing signs and wonders brought about by a man who is essentially the focus of the service time. Some of these men will actually blow on people to knock them backwards into the waiting arms of attendants, as if the Holy Spirit is some mystical force that can be blown from the mouth on command. Jesus described those who ran after signs and wonders as evil and adulterous (Matthew 12:39), because it implies that a person can only truly believe if they are given a physical sign or miracle by God. How blessed are those who have not seen Jesus, yet they love Him and believe in Him (1 Peter 1:8). Perhaps that is why Jesus declared, "Because you have seen Me, have you believed? Blessed are they who did not see, and yet believed" (John 20:29).

The Latest Craze?

Recently, a new practice has emerged in Canada referred to as the "Toronto Blessing," characterized in part by "holy laughter." The *Christian Research Journal* estimated that over 100,000 people have made a pilgrimage to the Toronto Airport Christian Fellowship to seek this experience. When asked, "What is it?" a pastor at the church commented, "I don't know, but isn't it wonderful?"

The practical guidelines of 1 Corinthians chapters 12 and 14 are nullified and teaching from God's Word has been impossible to carry out over the tumultuous noise of this phenomenon. If a practice would keep believers from hearing the Word of God, how can it be from the Holy Spirit? Why would the Holy Spirit hinder the hearing of His own Word? Yet pastors and congregations are flocking to join in. A large church in Anaheim, California recently hosted a Toronto Blessing conference called, "Let the Fire Fall." Over 5,000 people attended. In the late 1980's, people who howled and laughed hysterically at revival meetings in Argentina were taken outside the stadiums to have demons cast out. It is ironic that now raucous howling and uncontrollable laughter are considered by some as evidence of the Holy Spirit working in the life of the believer.

The Enemy's Confusion

The enemy can also cause confusion by distorting the person, attributes, and work of the Holy Spirit in the church. The Holy Spirit is often thought of as a force or essence, but the Bible teaches that He is a Person and is fully God. Some churches will use the worship time to "pump up" the congregation so that the Holy Spirit can then come, as if He is outside the room waiting for His cue to enter the sanctuary. Perhaps this is why many churches will say that the Spirit *really* came at one particular service, but not so at another, as if the Holy Spirit comes sometimes and then takes time off from some worship services. This is a wrong understanding of the person and work of the Holy Spirit.

The Holy Spirit is always present in the lives of believers, residing in the spiritual temple. The real question is whether people will allow Him that full place in their lives. The only true evidence of the Holy Spirit is God's *agape* love in the lives of believers. Evidence of the Holy Spirit is not based upon aerobic hype or emotion.

The enemy can also come in and confuse the body through lyrics that purport ideas about God that are not true. There are some lyrics that are somewhat easy to recognize as being contradictory to God's Word. However, there are more subtle means by which Satan can sow seeds of falsehood through erroneous lyrical content.

What would your response be to a song titled, "He Will Atone for Me?" At first glance the lyrics speak of Jesus' death and shed blood as the covering for our sins. But a more careful discernment reveals that the song presents the doctrine that Jesus must be sacrificed daily in the mass to make a continuous atonement for the sins of man. The Bible says that there is no longer a need for daily sacrifice because Christ made atonement (past tense) *once* for all when He offered (past tense) Himself on the cross (Hebrews 7:27 and 9:28). As another example, think about the song titled, "Awake Oh God Within Me." A careful examination of the verses and chorus reveals that this song encourages people to realize their own potential for being god-like. The lyrics do not speak of the Holy Spirit dwelling in man, but rather the very lie that Satan offered Eve in the garden.

Think of the spiritual damage that could be inflicted on a church body that comes together and lifts up images of God or ideas about God that are not consistent with what God has to say about Himself in His Word. There can exist a tendency to avoid being critical of lyric content; after all, musicians are artists who are involved in free expression. But real freedom comes in operating under the authority of the Bible, because it is sharper than any two-edged sword for the dividing of truth from falsehood (Hebrews 4:12) and is profitable for teaching, reproof, correction, and training in righteousness (2 Timothy 3:16).

Some composers may feel cramped by the Word of God, because it does not allow for the *spirit* to have freedom to inspire. The response to this needs to always be, to what spirit should freedom be given, man's spirit or God's? Freedom under the Holy Spirit will never produce a contradiction with God's Word. Remember, all Scripture is God-breathed. Paul correctly admonished the church in Corinth that if any of them thought they were a prophet or spiritual, they could check out what they had to say by simply comparing it to God's own commandments written in the Scriptures (1 Corinthians 14:37). Paul urged the church to keep an eye out for dissensions and hindrances contrary to the true teaching which they learned, and to turn away from these (Romans 16:17). Each word that is spoken and each lyric that is sung during the time of worship must support and blend with the message of the sermon and the content of the time in prayer. Together these will produce a message that is wholly consistent with the Word of God.

The Enemy's Competition

Spiritual warfare can also take place within, and between, the people involved in leading worship. Jesus said that envy, pride, and deeds of covetousness come out of the heart (Mark 7:22). These are the same basic areas where Satan fell into rebellion against God, and pride is not from God but from the world (1 John 2:16). To have envy, is to grudge the position or blessing of someone else. It is mentioned eight times in the New Testament, generally in the same context of pride, jealousy, and covetousness. The high priests in Jerusalem were jealous of the attention that the apostles received from the multitudes who came to hear the gospel message (Acts 5:17).

Musicians are very susceptible to feelings of pride in their own talent and accomplishments, as well as jealousy, envy, and covetousness toward the accomplishments of others. Proverbs 27:19 states that the heart of a man reflects who a man actually is. A worship leader may be a relatively high-profile position within the church. The person leading worship is in front of the congregation and will have the opportunity to demonstrate skills in singing and playing a musical instrument. It can be very easy for that person to enjoy the attention of the people. There can sometimes be applause and recognition from the audience in response to sharing musical gifts. This opens the door for pride to move in.

God knew that man would have a problem coveting what was not his (Exodus 20:17). A musician can covet the position and authority of a worship leader, or be jealous of another individual's skill level on an instrument or in vocal talent. A person could envy another's song-writing ability. Music ministry will involve personal tastes and preferences that vary from musician to musician.

Some individuals can tend to be perfectionists when it comes to vocal harmonies or the arrangement dynamics of worship songs. The time just prior to the worship service (while instruments are tuned and microphone levels are set) can be dominated by attitudes and agendas that are from the flesh of man and not from the Spirit of the living God. Too often, these carry over into the worship time as well. When pride, covetousness, and jealousy are present there is usually a lack of submission to authority. Without humble hearts and submission to leadership, the worship of God will lack the necessary components of *spirit* and *truth*, and be distracted away from God and toward man. Strife on the music team is generally not a matter of "personality conflicts." It is spiritual in nature and must be handled through the covering of prayer and submission to the authority of the Holy Spirit.

CHAPTER 7

WORSHIP AND THE GIFTS OF THE HOLY SPIRIT

Worship and music ministry will always be intimately connected with the manifestation by the Holy Spirit of various types of spiritual gifts. Worship is a spiritual matter. The gifts are also a spiritual matter and given by God as He wills (Hebrews 2:4). There is one Spirit who works all things, distributing gifts to each one individually just as He wills (1 Corinthians 12:11). The twelfth principle is that: ***Worship and the Gifts Will Work Together Under the Leading and Direction of the Holy Spirit.***

A basic starting point by which to examine and build upon this aspect of music ministry is the fourteenth chapter of Paul's first letter to the church in Corinth. The Holy Spirit wanted that

church to know that there is a specific outcome
of the work of the Holy Spirit. When the church
body assembles together for a service, "each one
has a psalm, has a teaching, has a revelation, has
a tongue, has an interpretation." All these things
are done for the edification of everyone present.
Edification literally means "house" or
"structure." We get our word *edifice* from the
same root word. The gifts of the Holy Spirit are
ultimately intended to bring about the worship
of God. For instance, the Bible teaches that a
spoken word of prophecy discloses the secrets of
the listener's heart so that the one who hears it
will fall on his face and *worship* God (1
Corinthians 14:25).

Our Words and Our Worship

The Bible describes five specific gifts that are
outward manifestations of the Holy Spirit. These
gifts are intended for the encouragement of the
entire assembly of believers (1 Corinthians 14).
The first gift mentioned is a "psalm," or *psalmos*
in the Greek. This is literally translated as a
"piece of music" and is generally referred to in
the Bible in the context of praise, often with the
term *humnos*, a hymn. It is also associated with
the *pneumatikos oide*, or spiritual song (these

were previously reviewed in chapter 2). Christian composers can rest in the confidence that the Holy Spirit is the source and the basis for each "piece of music" (psalm) and the lyrics that come with it. The Bible clearly states that what we receive is not the spirit of the world, but the Holy Spirit who is from God; that we might know the things freely given to us by God, which we also speak, not in words taught by human wisdom, but by the Spirit, combining spiritual thoughts with spiritual words (1 Corinthians 2:13). True worship music is inspired by the Holy Spirit and music inspired by the Holy Spirit will always be true to God's Word.

A Place for Sound Doctrine

A second gift present during the church gathering is the *didache*. This is where we get our word *doctrine* and literally means "a teaching or specific instruction." The Holy Spirit will teach all those in whom He dwells (1 John 2:27). Those in the early church continually devoted themselves to the apostle's *didache* (Acts 2:42). Believers are to be ready in season and out of season to reprove, rebuke, and exhort based on doctrine, or *didache* (2 Timothy 4:2), and this must be sound in content (Titus 1:9). Christians should not be carried away by poor doctrine (Hebrews 13:9 and 2 John 1:10).

The third gift for the church service time is the *apokalupsis*, or literally the "disclosure." This is provided to the body of Christ by the Holy Spirit for the purpose of identifying specific areas of exhortation and admonition. This word is used 17 times in the New Testament and always speaks of "revealing" something. Paul addresses potential problems with this *apokalupsis* and with visions, because they can be abused (2 Corinthians 12:1). In the Greek, "visions" is *optasia*, from the same root where we get the word "optical." Obviously, great care must be taken to discern when someone is truly speaking a revelation or seeing a vision.

A Heavenly Word

A fourth gift for the church assembly is the *glossa* or "tongue." This involves a spoken word in a language directed at a person or persons for their ears to hear. In that God wants everyone present to be edified through all that takes place in a congregational setting, the fifth item, the *hermeneia*, must always accompany the *glossa*. This is the "translation" or "interpretation" of the *glossa*. These five things taken together as a composite are intended to bring about a great work of God in the church, the *ginomai oikodome*, which means to "cause to become a structure or building." As mentioned before, the word *edification* has the same root as our word *edifice*, which is the outward or front portion of a building or structure. It is that which is built up first.

The Holy Spirit is the only one who has charge over how the gifts are used and manifested in the church. The Bible clearly teaches that, to one is given the word of wisdom through the Spirit, and to another the word of knowledge according to the same Spirit; to another faith by the same Spirit, and to another gifts of healing by the one Spirit, and to another the effecting of miracles, and to another prophecy, and to another the distinguishing of spirits, to another various kinds of tongues, and to another the interpretation of tongues (see 1 Corinthians chapters 12 and 14).

The gifts of the Holy Spirit can be thought of in three groups. First, there are gifts in which the Holy Spirit uses the spoken word. These include speaking a word of prophecy, speaking in a tongue, and speaking the interpretation of a tongue. Second, there are gifts that involve an action, which include both healing and accomplishing miracles. Third, the Holy Spirit uses the mind of an individual to communicate either a discerning of spirits, a measure of special wisdom, a word of knowledge, or a supernatural capacity for faith.

The Holy Spirit urges all believers to not be children in thinking, but to be mature in these specific matters of the gifts (see 1 Corinthians 14:20 and following). Paul recalled for the Corinthians that the prophet Isaiah foreknew that God would communicate to His people by His Spirit through the strange tongues and the lips of strangers, but that often they will not listen (Isaiah 28:11). The *glossa* makes no sense to the listener. Tongues do not hold much value as a tool for evangelism, unless it is to communicate the gospel message to a people whose language was outside the capacity of the one speaking to them. Tongues are not presented in the Bible within the context of preaching the gospel message. Even at Pentecost, only Peter preached (and that was in his own language) while the others who spoke in various foreign tongues were rejoicing and praising God, to the extent that they were thought to be drunk (see 1 Corinthians 14:23–24).

In a similar manner, prophecy is intended for believers, for those who *will* listen and be obedient to the word of the Lord. The Holy Spirit can use music to communicate deep, personal praises to God, and these are consistent with the basis for the gifts of the Holy Spirit and God's Word.

Our Words Set to Music

Music can clearly communicate a message for the edification of all who assemble together. Music can express praises to God. It can transmit the gospel message to unbelievers as a declaration of God's plan of salvation. It can be directed to the Holy Spirit, or to share something of deep personal value so as to encourage and build up the body of believers who are listening. When music and worship are examined in conjunction with the working of the gifts of the Holy Spirit, they do not contradict or hinder each other, but they support and complement each other with a single purpose, to bring about a closer relationship between God and man.

CHAPTER 8

WORSHIP AND THE FELLOWSHIP OF BELIEVERS

Music has great value in the context of the fellowship of believers. This is where all of the preceding chapters come together. The entire basis for this concept of "the church" (the "body of Christ") might well be centered on the Bible's teaching of the fellowship of believers. The Greek word for fellowship is *koinonia*, which literally means communion, participation, or intimacy. This *koinonia* is described throughout the New Testament. Whether in building up one another (the edifice) or in taking the message of God's salvation to those who have not heard the Good News, the mutual participation and communion of those of kindred spirit creates an exceptional basis for the body of Christ.

The thirteenth principle is that: ***Worship Will Develop and Sustain a Strong and Lasting Fellowship Within the Church.*** The Bible specifically describes distinct types of *koinonia*. These are significant because they remove the possibility that any single group could have a "lock on" the exclusive rights to fellowship. There is first the *koinonia* with the Father. There is also distinct communion with the Son, Jesus Christ. A third unique fellowship exists with the Holy Spirit. And there is also described a *koinonia* with other believers.

Various Types of Fellowship

The first type of specific fellowship is with God the Father and is spoken of in John's Gospel (chapter 1:5). "And this is the message we have heard from Him and announce to you, that God is light, and in Him there is no darkness at all. If we say that we have *fellowship with Him (God)* and yet walk in the darkness, we lie and do not practice the truth." Paul conveys a second and unique nature of fellowship, that of believers with Jesus Christ. He notes that God is faithful, and it is through God, that believers are called into "...*fellowship with His Son, Jesus Christ our Lord*" (1 Corinthians 1:9). This close communion has a third distinction, in the believer's relationship with the Holy Spirit as well. There is a separate effect between "the grace of the Lord Jesus Christ, and the love of God, and *the fellowship of the Holy Spirit*," which is to be with all believers (2 Corinthians 13:14).

Paul amplified certain obvious truths to make a point about the need for believers to be one in purpose (Philippians 2:2). Preceding this, he asked rhetorically if there was any encouragement in Christ (which he knew there was) and then if there was any consolation of love (which he also knew there was). He then asked if there were any *fellowship* of the Spirit, any affection, any compassion. He again was making clear the indisputable fact that there most certainly is a distinct *koinonia* of the Spirit.

The Bible teaches a fourth type of *koinonia*, clearly stating that if we as believers walk in the light as He Himself is in the light, we have fellowship with one another, and the blood of Jesus, His Son, cleanses us from all sin (1 John 1:7). Accounts of the early church report that believers "were continually devoting themselves to the apostles' teaching and to *koinonia* (fellowship), and to the breaking of bread and to prayer" (Acts 2:42).

God's Word declares that there is an expected outcome from this fellowship of believers. When believers assemble together, each person should have a psalm (song), a teaching, a revelation, a tongue and an interpretation, and all for the edification of the entire church body (1 Corinthians 14:26). This is important because the Holy Spirit later witnesses that some individuals in the early church had rejected this interaction (Hebrews 10:25). The church body is strongly exhorted to not forsake the assembling together, as had become the habit of some, but they were to encourage one another. Why was this important? The text continues that it was crucial and substantive all the more as they saw the day drawing near. The day that was referred to was that point in time when Jesus would come for His bride, the church.

The New Testament refers many times to His coming to take His church out of the world before the judgment as "the blessed hope" of all those who believe. Notice that in the instruction to not forsake assembling together the Holy

Spirit says that this had become a habit for many. The Greek word used for habit is *ethos*, which means a deep-rooted custom or manner. Apart from God, and in our flesh, each of us is susceptible to slipping into a similarly deep-rooted custom of avoiding fellowship with the body of Christ. Many people in the church today have filled Sunday morning with other activities to avoid worship and hearing the Word of God.

Paul records an interesting fifth category of *koinonia*, or communion, in the gospel message itself. The Spirit directs him to write of their *"participation* (koinonia) in the gospel from the first day until now"* (Philippians 1:5). Believers fellowship in the good news of the salvation message. When the church body comes together in worship and teaching from God's Word, and it is all under the authority and direction of the Holy Spirit, fellowship takes place. We experience communion and intimacy with God. This is the ultimate purpose of worship and the gifts of the Spirit, to build one another into a spiritual house for a holy priesthood, to offer up spiritual sacrifices acceptable to God through Jesus Christ (1 Peter 2:5).

Fellowship to Remember Christ

When Jesus ate the last Passover dinner with
His disciples just prior to His death on the cross,
He knew that these men would, for a few years
to come, be enjoying fellowship together again
after He would return to heaven. He inferred in
the broader context of His statement that all
those in the future who would assemble
together in His name should remember His new
covenant by eating the unleavened bread and
drinking of the fruit of the vine (see Luke 22 and
1 Corinthians 11). He was careful to note that a
man should first examine himself before taking
the bread and the cup, because he who eats and
drinks, eats and drinks judgment to himself, if
he does not judge the body rightly.

What exactly was the church to remember
when they celebrated the Passover in the new
covenant setting? A person who knows Jesus
Christ as Savior would know Him, and know
the power of His resurrection, and also know the
koinonia of His sufferings, and that these would
come about as the believer was conformed to
His death (see Philippians 3). This fellowship of
His sufferings is also confirmed in the letter to
the church in Rome. Paul told the Roman

believers that if they had all been baptized into Christ Jesus, they had also been baptized into His death (Romans 6:3). This is an interesting way to participate (fellowship) in His sufferings, and would accomplish an extraordinary occurrence in the life of each individual. The church in Corinth was also made aware that the cup of blessing was a *koinonia* in the blood of Christ, and the bread was a *koinonia* in the body of Christ (1 Corinthians 10:16).

The Bible clearly teaches that there can be no *koinonia* between light and darkness. John contrasts these, in such that no partnership exists for righteousness and lawlessness, and there is no *koinonia* between light and darkness (e.g., John 1:4–9; 3:20–21; 1 John 1:7). It is a principle that can be proven with a match and a closet. When the door is shut, the closet is pitch dark and no light exists. It is impossible to see. When the match is lit, light is introduced and the darkness retreats. They cannot coexist.

EPILOGUE

The closing principle is that: *True Worship of God Will Nurture True Spiritual Life.* True spiritual life will not come by running after signs and wonders. It will not be found in "the latest craze" to spring up at some church somewhere. True spiritual life is resting in the promises of God, secure in a knowledge of Him, and being filled continually with the Holy Spirit unto good works and fellowship with God, His Son, and with the Holy Spirit. May God grant us the humility and maturity to not stray away from Him, but to hold fast to Him and to His Word until He brings us to the marriage supper of the Lamb, when we will meet the Lord in the air and thus we shall be with Him for eternity (1 Thessalonians 4:17), where we shall see Him face to face (1 Corinthians 13:12), we will know that we ran the race well (Hebrews 12:1), and we will hopefully hear Him say, "Well done, My good and faithful servant, enter into the joy of your Master" (Matthew 25).

To summarize our principles, the Bible teaches that a clear knowledge of God's Word will cause people to worship God as a heartfelt response to knowing Him. When the time for worship is covered in prayer and treated with the same preparation as the teaching from God's Word, God will bless His people as they bless Him through their worship. God alone is the only One worthy to be worshipped, and He commands that those who wish to worship Him must do so in spirit and in truth. God has gifted the church with beautiful music to be used in worship of Him, and He has specifically called people in the church to serve as worship leaders for God's people. The worship of God is really service to God. Those who lead worship must have the heart of a servant.

Worship must always be in truth, relative to God's Word. The music that is used for worship must be wholly consistent with all that the Bible teaches about God. And while there may be slight differences in music preference or the style of lyrics employed, the substantive content of worship must have no variation, and the basis for the worship is the Word of God.

Worship is inherently a spiritual matter, therefore believers should know that there will always be spiritual warfare associated with the worship of God. This conflict dates back to the original sin of Satan, when he coveted the position and authority of God. Counterfeit worship can distract and hinder the work of the Holy Spirit. True worship will never contradict God's Word or hinder people from hearing, and responding to, God's Word.

The gifts of the Holy Spirit are also a spiritual matter. The gifts will always work in perfect harmony with the worship of God, as the Holy Spirit directs the hearts of men in the praise of God. The result of the gifts is that everyone would be edified, or built up, in their knowledge and love of God. The ultimate consequence of the working of the Holy Spirit through the worship and the gifts, is that there will be koinonia among the church body. This koinonia is true fellowship and participation together with God in all that Christ has accomplished in His finished work on the cross.

This book has touched on numerous issues that are related to the worship of God and the role of music ministry in the church. It was never intended to be a comprehensive analysis of every possible situation that might arise within the church concerning worship and music ministry. The entire subject matter in these areas is certainly more extensive than these pages can review. However, there are specific topics that exist at the core of worship and music ministry that are foundational in nature. The 14 principles offered in this book were designed to provide a primary basis for understanding the way worship and music ministry impact the spiritual life of the church. There are clear teachings in the Bible that directly pertain to the worship of God and involvement in music ministry.

The Holy Spirit has instructed the church to "see to it that no one takes you captive through philosophy and empty deception, according to the tradition of men, according to the elementary principles of the world, rather than according to Christ" (Colossians 2:8). There are basic principles by which the world operates, and these are not founded in God's truth, but rather in man's ideas and inclinations. The church is instructed to die to the world's thinking (Colossians 2:20). God wants His people to have understanding in spiritual matters and He calls His church to be taught the elementary principles of the oracles of God (Hebrews 5:12). Perhaps this book can be a starting point from which worship and music ministry can be better understood in light of God's Word. May God richly bless us all until we see Him face to face.

How to Become a Christian

First of all you must recognize that you are a sinner. Realize that you have missed the mark. This is true of each of us. We have deliberately crossed the line not once, but many times. The Bible says, *"All have sinned and fallen short of the glory of God"* (Romans 3:23). This is a hard admission for many to make, but if we are not willing to hear the bad news, we cannot appreciate and respond to the *good news*.

Second, we must realize that Jesus Christ died on the cross for us. Because of sin, God had to take drastic measures to reach us. So He came to this earth and walked here as a man. But Jesus was more than just a good man. He was the God-man—God incarnate—and that is why His death on the cross is so significant.

At the cross, God Himself—in the person of Jesus Christ—took our place and bore our sins. He paid for them and purchased our redemption.

Third, we must repent of our sin. God has commanded men everywhere to repent. Acts 3:19 states, *"Repent therefore and be converted, that your sins may be blotted out, so that times of refreshing may come from the presence of the Lord."* What does this word *repent* mean? It means to change direction–to hang a U-turn on the road of life. It means to stop living the kind of life we led previously and start living the kind of life outlined in the pages of the Bible. Now we must change and be willing to make a break with the past.

Fourth, we must receive Jesus Christ into our hearts and lives. Being a Christian is having God Himself take residence in our lives. John 1:12 tells us, *"But as many as received Him, to them He gave the right to become children of God."* We must receive Him. Jesus said, *"Behold, I stand at the door and knock. If anyone hears My voice and opens the door, I will come in..."* (Revelation 3:20). Each one of us must individually decide to open the door. How do we open it? Through prayer.

If you have never asked Jesus Christ to come into your life, you can do it right now. Here is a suggested prayer you might even pray.

Lord Jesus, I know that I am a sinner and I am sorry for my sin. I turn and repent of my sins right now. Thank You for dying on the cross for me and paying the price for my sin. Please come into my heart and life right now. Fill me with Your Holy Spirit and help me to be Your disciple. Thank You for forgiving me and coming into my life. Thank You that I am now a child of Yours and that I am going to heaven. In Jesus' name, I pray. Amen.

When you pray that prayer God will respond. You have made the right decision–the decision that will impact how you spend eternity. Now you will go to heaven, and in the meantime, find peace and the answers to your spiritual questions.

Taken from: *Life. Any Questions?*
by Greg Laurie, Copyright © 1995. Used by permission.

Other books available in this series...

Spiritual Warfare
by Brian Brodersen

Pastor Brian Brodersen of Calvary Chapel Westminster, England brings biblical balance and practical insight to the subject of spiritual warfare.

The Psychologizing of the Faith
by Bob Hoekstra

Pastor Bob Hoekstra of Living in Christ Ministries calls the church to leave the broken cisterns of human wisdom, and to return to the fountain of living water flowing from our wonderful counselor, Jesus Christ.

Practical Christian Living
by Wayne Taylor

Pastor Wayne Taylor of Calvary Fellowship in Seattle, Washington takes us through a study of Romans 12 and 13 showing us what practical Christian living is all about.

Building Godly Character
by Ray Bentley

Pastor Ray Bentley of Maranatha Chapel in San Diego, California takes us through a study in the life of David to show how God builds His character in our individual lives.

Worship and Music Ministry
by Rick Ryan & Dave Newton

Pastor Rick Ryan and Dave Newton of Calvary Chapel Santa Barbara, California give us solid biblical insight into the very important subjects of worship and ministering to the body of Christ through music.

Overcoming Sin & Enjoying God
by Danny Bond
Pastor Danny Bond of Pacific Hills Church in Aliso Viejo, California shows us, through practical principles, that it is possible to live in victory over sin and have constant fellowship with our loving God.

Answers for the Skeptic
by Scott Richards
Pastor Scott Richards of Calvary Fellowship in Tucson, Arizona shows us what to say when our faith is challenged, and how to answer the skeptic in a way that opens hearts to the love and truth of Jesus Christ.

Effective Prayer Life
by Chuck Smith
Pastor Chuck Smith of Calvary Chapel of Costa Mesa, California discusses the principles of prayer, the keys to having a dynamic prayer life, and the victorious results of such a life. It will stir in your heart a desire to "pray without ceasing."

Creation by Design
by Mark Eastman, M.D.
Mark Eastman, M.D., of Genesis Outreach in Temecula, California carefully examines and clarifies the evidence for a Creator God, and the reality of His relationship to mankind.

The Afterglow
by Henry Gainey
Pastor Henry Gainey of Calvary Chapel Thomasville, Georgia gives instruction in conducting and understanding the proper use of the gifts of the Holy Spirit in an "Afterglow Service."

Final Curtain
by Chuck Smith
Pastor Chuck Smith of Calvary Chapel Costa Mesa,
California provides insight into God's prophetic plan and
shows how current events are leading to the time when one
climactic battle will usher in eternity.

For ordering information, please contact:
The Word For Today
P.O. Box 8000, Costa Mesa, CA 92628
(800) 272-WORD
Also, visit us on the Internet at:
www.thewordfortoday.org